Book and Audio for B♭, E♭, C and Bass Clef Instruments

JAZZ FUNK

volume 178

Arranged and Produced by Mark Taylor and Jim Roberts

PLAYBACK+
Speed • Pitch • Balance • Loop

T0079485

To access audio visit:
www.halleonard.com/mylibrary

Enter Code
5677-3471-5954-6210

ISBN 978-1-4803-5356-5

HAL•LEONARD® CORPORATION

7777 W. BLUEMOUND RD. P.O. BOX 13819 MILWAUKEE, WI 53213

Visit Hal Leonard Online at
www.halleonard.com

JAZZ/FUNK

Volume 178

Arranged and Produced
Mark Taylor and Jim Roberts

Featured Players:

Graham Breedlove–Trumpet
John Desalme–Sax
Tony Nalker–Piano
Jim Roberts–Guitar
Paul Henry–Bass
Todd Harrison–Drums

Recorded at Bias Studios, Springfield, Virginia
Bob Dawson, Engineer

HOW TO USE THE AUDIO:

Each song has two tracks:

1) Split Track/Melody

Woodwind, Brass, Keyboard, and **Mallet Players** can use
this track as a learning tool for melody style and inflection.

Bass Players can learn and perform with this track –
remove the recorded bass track by turning down the
volume on the LEFT channel.

Keyboard and **Guitar Players** can learn and perform with
this track – remove the recorded piano part by turning down
the volume on the RIGHT channel.

2) Full Stereo Track

Soloists or **Groups** can learn and perform with this
accompaniment track with the RHYTHM SECTION only.

Always There

WORDS AND MUSIC BY RONNIE LAWS,
WILLIAM JEFFREY AND PAUL ALLEN

C VERSION

THE CHICKEN

BY ALFRED ELLIS

C Version

CISSY STRUT

BY ARTHUR NEVILLE, LEO NOCENTELLI,
GEORGE PORTER AND JOSEPH MODELISTE, JR.

C VERSION

Compared to What

WORDS AND MUSIC BY
EUGENE MCDANIELS

C VERSION

LISTEN HERE

BY EDDIE HARRIS

C VERSION

PUT IT WHERE YOU WANT IT

BY JOE SAMPLE

C VERSION

Sookie Sookie

WORDS AND MUSIC BY
STEVE CROPPER AND DON COVAY

C VERSION

WESTCHESTER LADY

BY BOB JAMES

C VERSION

WINELIGHT

WORDS AND MUSIC BY
WILLIAM EATON

C VERSION

Always There

WORDS AND MUSIC BY RONNIE LAWS,
WILLIAM JEFFREY AND PAUL ALLEN

THE CHICKEN

BY ALFRED ELLIS

Bb VERSION

CISSY STRUT

BY ARTHUR NEVILLE, LEO NOCENTELLI,
GEORGE PORTER AND JOSEPH MODELISTE, JR.

Bb Version

Compared to What

WORDS AND MUSIC BY
EUGENE MCDANIELS

LISTEN HERE

BY EDDIE HARRIS

PUT IT WHERE YOU WANT IT

BY JOE SAMPLE

Bb VERSION

Sookie Sookie

WORDS AND MUSIC BY
STEVE CROPPER AND DON COVAY

Bb Version

WESTCHESTER LADY

BY BOB JAMES

Bb VERSION

WINELIGHT

WORDS AND MUSIC BY
WILLIAM EATON

Bb VERSION

Always There

Words and Music by Ronnie Laws,
William Jeffrey and Paul Allen

Eb Version

THE CHICKEN

BY ALFRED ELLIS

Eb VERSION

MEDIUM FUNK

CISSY STRUT

BY ARTHUR NEVILLE, LEO NOCENTELLI,
GEORGE PORTER AND JOSEPH MODELISTE, JR.

Compared to What

Words and Music by
Eugene McDaniels

Eb Version

LISTEN HERE

BY EDDIE HARRIS

Eb VERSION

PUT IT WHERE YOU WANT IT

BY JOE SAMPLE

Eb VERSION

Sookie Sookie

WORDS AND MUSIC BY
STEVE CROPPER AND DON COVAY

WESTCHESTER LADY

BY BOB JAMES

Eb VERSION

WINELIGHT

WORDS AND MUSIC BY
WILLIAM EATON

Always There

WORDS AND MUSIC BY RONNIE LAWS,
WILLIAM JEFFREY AND PAUL ALLEN

THE CHICKEN

BY ALFRED ELLIS

CISSY STRUT

BY ARTHUR NEVILLE, LEO NOCENTELLI,
GEORGE PORTER AND JOSEPH MODELISTE, JR.

COMPARED TO WHAT

WORDS AND MUSIC BY
EUGENE MCDANIELS

LISTEN HERE

BY EDDIE HARRIS

PUT IT WHERE YOU WANT IT

BY JOE SAMPLE

SOOKIE SOOKIE

WORDS AND MUSIC BY
STEVE CROPPER AND DON COVAY

WESTCHESTER LADY

BY BOB JAMES

WINELIGHT

WORDS AND MUSIC BY
WILLIAM EATON

Presenting the Hal Leonard JAZZ PLAY-ALONG® SERIES

For use with all B-flat, E-flat, Bass Clef and C instruments, the Jazz Play-Along® Series is the ultimate learning tool for all jazz musicians. With musician-friendly lead sheets, melody cues, and other split-track audio choices included, these first-of-a-kind packages help you master improvisation while playing some of the greatest tunes of all time. FOR STUDY, each tune includes a split track with: melody cue with proper style and inflection • professional rhythm tracks • choruses for soloing • removable bass part • removable piano part. FOR PERFORMANCE, each tune also has: an additional full stereo accompaniment track (no melody) • additional choruses for soloing.

1A. MAIDEN VOYAGE/ALL BLUES
00843158 .... $22.99

1. DUKE ELLINGTON
00841644.. $16.99

2. MILES DAVIS
00841645.. $17.99

3. THE BLUES
00841646.. $19.99

4. JAZZ BALLADS
00841691.. $17.99

5. BEST OF BEBOP
00841689.. $17.99

6. JAZZ CLASSICS WITH EASY CHANGES
00841690.. $16.99

7. ESSENTIAL JAZZ STANDARDS
00843000.. $17.99

8. ANTONIO CARLOS JOBIM AND THE ART OF THE BOSSA NOVA
00843001.. $16.99

9. DIZZY GILLESPIE
00843002.. $19.99

10. DISNEY CLASSICS
00843003.. $16.99

12. ESSENTIAL JAZZ CLASSICS
00843005.. $16.99

13. JOHN COLTRANE
00843006.. $17.99

14. IRVING BERLIN
00843007.. $16.99

15. RODGERS & HAMMERSTEIN
00843008.. $16.99

16. COLE PORTER
00843009.. $17.99

17. COUNT BASIE
00843010.. $17.99

18. HAROLD ARLEN
00843011.. $17.99

20. CHRISTMAS CAROLS
00843080.. $16.99

21. RODGERS AND HART CLASSICS
00843014.. $16.99

22. WAYNE SHORTER
00843015.. $17.99

23. LATIN JAZZ
00843016.. $19.99

24. EARLY JAZZ STANDARDS
00843017.. $16.99

25. CHRISTMAS JAZZ
00843018.. $17.99

26. CHARLIE PARKER
00843019.. $16.99

27. GREAT JAZZ STANDARDS
00843020.. $17.99

28. BIG BAND ERA
00843021.. $17.99

29. LENNON AND MCCARTNEY
00843022.. $24.99

30. BLUES' BEST
00843023.. $16.99

31. JAZZ IN THREE
00843024.. $16.99

32. BEST OF SWING
00843025.. $17.99

33. SONNY ROLLINS
00843029.. $16.99

34. ALL TIME STANDARDS
00843030.. $17.99

35. BLUESY JAZZ
00843031.. $17.99

36. HORACE SILVER
00843032.. $19.99

37. BILL EVANS
00843033.. $16.99

38. YULETIDE JAZZ
00843034.. $16.99

39. "ALL THE THINGS YOU ARE" & MORE JEROME KERN SONGS
00843035.. $19.99

40. BOSSA NOVA
00843036.. $19.99

41. CLASSIC DUKE ELLINGTON
00843037.. $16.99

42. GERRY MULLIGAN FAVORITES
00843038.. $16.99

43. GERRY MULLIGAN CLASSICS
00843039.. $19.99

45. GEORGE GERSHWIN
00103643.. $24.99

47. CLASSIC JAZZ BALLADS
00843043.. $17.99

48. BEBOP CLASSICS
00843044.. $16.99

49. MILES DAVIS STANDARDS
00843045.. $19.99

52. STEVIE WONDER
00843048.. $17.99

53. RHYTHM CHANGES
00843049.. $16.99

55. BENNY GOLSON
00843052.. $19.99

56. "GEORGIA ON MY MIND" & OTHER SONGS BY HOAGY CARMICHAEL
00843056.. $17.99

57. VINCE GUARALDI
00843057.. $16.99

58. MORE LENNON AND MCCARTNEY
00843059.. $17.99

59. SOUL JAZZ
00843060.. $17.99

60. DEXTER GORDON
00843061.. $16.99

61. MONGO SANTAMARIA
00843062.. $16.99

62. JAZZ-ROCK FUSION
00843063.. $19.99

63. CLASSICAL JAZZ
00843064.. $16.99

64. TV TUNES
00843065.. $16.99

65. SMOOTH JAZZ
00843066.. $19.99

66. A CHARLIE BROWN CHRISTMAS
00843067.. $16.99

67. CHICK COREA
00843068.. $22.99

68. CHARLES MINGUS
00843069.. $19.99

71. COLE PORTER CLASSICS
00843073.. $16.99

72. CLASSIC JAZZ BALLADS
00843074.. $16.99

73. JAZZ/BLUES
00843075.. $16.99

74. BEST JAZZ CLASSICS
00843076.. $16.99

75. PAUL DESMOND
00843077.. $17.99

78. STEELY DAN
00843070.. $19.99

79. MILES DAVIS CLASSICS
00843081.. $16.99

80. JIMI HENDRIX
00843083.. $17.99

83. ANDREW LLOYD WEBBER
00843104.. $16.99

84. BOSSA NOVA CLASSICS
00843105.. $17.99

85. MOTOWN HITS
00843109.. $17.99

86. BENNY GOODMAN
00843110.. $17.99

87. DIXIELAND
00843111.. $16.99

90. **THELONIOUS MONK CLASSICS**
00841262 ....$16.99

91. **THELONIOUS MONK FAVORITES**
00841263 ....$17.99

92. **LEONARD BERNSTEIN**
00450134 ....$16.99

93. **DISNEY FAVORITES**
00843142 ....$16.99

94. **RAY**
00843143 ....$19.99

95. **JAZZ AT THE LOUNGE**
00843144 ....$17.99

96. **LATIN JAZZ STANDARDS**
00843145 ....$16.99

97. **MAYBE I'M AMAZED***
00843148 ....$16.99

98. **DAVE FRISHBERG**
00843149 ....$16.99

99. **SWINGING STANDARDS**
00843150 ....$16.99

100. **LOUIS ARMSTRONG**
00740423 ....$19.99

101. **BUD POWELL**
00843152 ....$16.99

102. **JAZZ POP**
00843153 ....$19.99

103. **ON GREEN DOLPHIN STREET
& OTHER JAZZ CLASSICS**
00843154 ....$16.99

104. **ELTON JOHN**
00843155 ....$19.99

105. **SOULFUL JAZZ**
00843151 ....$17.99

106. **SLO' JAZZ**
00843117 ....$16.99

107. **MOTOWN CLASSICS**
00843116 ....$17.99

108. **JAZZ WALTZ**
00843159 ....$16.99

109. **OSCAR PETERSON**
00843160 ....$16.99

110. **JUST STANDARDS**
00843161 ....$16.99

111. **COOL CHRISTMAS**
00843162 ....$16.99

112. **PAQUITO D'RIVERA – LATIN JAZZ***
48020662 ....$16.99

113. **PAQUITO D'RIVERA – BRAZILIAN JAZZ***
48020663 ....$19.99

114. **MODERN JAZZ QUARTET FAVORITES**
00843163 ....$16.99

115. **THE SOUND OF MUSIC**
00843164 ....$16.99

116. **JACO PASTORIUS**
00843165 ....$17.99

117. **ANTONIO CARLOS JOBIM – MORE HITS**
00843166 ....$17.99

118. **BIG JAZZ STANDARDS COLLECTION**
00843167 ....$27.50

119. **JELLY ROLL MORTON**
00843168 ....$16.99

120. **J.S. BACH**
00843169 ....$17.99

121. **DJANGO REINHARDT**
00843170 ....$16.99

122. **PAUL SIMON**
00843182 ....$16.99

123. **BACHARACH & DAVID**
00843185 ....$16.99

124. **JAZZ-ROCK HORN HITS**
00843186 ....$16.99

125. **SAMMY NESTICO**
00843187 ....$16.99

126. **COUNT BASIE CLASSICS**
00843157 ....$16.99

127. **CHUCK MANGIONE**
00843188 ....$19.99

128. **VOCAL STANDARDS (LOW VOICE)**
00843189 ....$16.99

129. **VOCAL STANDARDS (HIGH VOICE)**
00843190 ....$16.99

130. **VOCAL JAZZ (LOW VOICE)**
00843191 ....$16.99

131. **VOCAL JAZZ (HIGH VOICE)**
00843192 ....$16.99

132. **STAN GETZ ESSENTIALS**
00843193 ....$17.99

133. **STAN GETZ FAVORITES**
00843194 ....$16.99

134. **NURSERY RHYMES***
00843196 ....$17.99

135. **JEFF BECK**
00843197 ....$16.99

136. **NAT ADDERLEY**
00843198 ....$16.99

137. **WES MONTGOMERY**
00843199 ....$16.99

138. **FREDDIE HUBBARD**
00843200 ....$16.99

139. **JULIAN "CANNONBALL" ADDERLEY**
00843201 ....$16.99

140. **JOE ZAWINUL**
00843202 ....$16.99

141. **BILL EVANS STANDARDS**
00843156 ....$16.99

142. **CHARLIE PARKER GEMS**
00843222 ....$16.99

143. **JUST THE BLUES**
00843223 ....$16.99

144. **LEE MORGAN**
00843229 ....$16.99

145. **COUNTRY STANDARDS**
00843230 ....$16.99

146. **RAMSEY LEWIS**
00843231 ....$16.99

147. **SAMBA**
00843232 ....$16.99

148. **JOHN COLTRANE FAVORITES**
00843233 ....$16.99

149. **JOHN COLTRANE – GIANT STEPS**
00843234 ....$16.99

150. **JAZZ IMPROV BASICS**
00843195 ....$19.99

151. **MODERN JAZZ QUARTET CLASSICS**
00843209 ....$16.99

152. **J.J. JOHNSON**
00843210 ....$16.99

153. **KENNY GARRETT**
00843212 ....$16.99

154. **HENRY MANCINI**
00843213 ....$17.99

155. **SMOOTH JAZZ CLASSICS**
00843215 ....$17.99

156. **THELONIOUS MONK – EARLY GEMS**
00843216 ....$16.99

157. **HYMNS**
00843217 ....$16.99

158. **JAZZ COVERS ROCK**
00843219 ....$16.99

159. **MOZART**
00843220 ....$16.99

160. **GEORGE SHEARING**
14041531 ....$16.99

161. **DAVE BRUBECK**
14041556 ....$16.99

162. **BIG CHRISTMAS COLLECTION**
00843221 ....$24.99

163. **JOHN COLTRANE STANDARDS**
00843235 ....$16.99

164. **HERB ALPERT**
14041775 ....$19.98

165. **GEORGE BENSON**
00843240 ....$17.99

166. **ORNETTE COLEMAN**
00843241 ....$16.99

167. **JOHNNY MANDEL**
00103642 ....$16.99

168. **TADD DAMERON**
00103663 ....$16.99

169. **BEST JAZZ STANDARDS**
00109249 ....$24.99

170. **ULTIMATE JAZZ STANDARDS**
00109250 ....$24.99

171. **RADIOHEAD**
00109305 ....$16.99

172. **POP STANDARDS**
00111669 ....$16.99

174. **TIN PAN ALLEY**
00119125 ....$16.99

175. **TANGO**
00119836 ....$16.99

176. **JOHNNY MERCER**
00119838 ....$16.99

177. **THE II-V-I PROGRESSION**
00843239 ....$24.99

178. **JAZZ/FUNK**
00121902 ....$17.99

179. **MODAL JAZZ**
00122273 ....$16.99

180. **MICHAEL JACKSON**
00122327 ....$17.99

181. **BILLY JOEL**
00122329 ....$19.99

182. **"RHAPSODY IN BLUE" & 7 OTHER
CLASSICAL-BASED JAZZ PIECES**
00116847 ....$16.99

183. **SONDHEIM**
00126253 ....$16.99

184. **JIMMY SMITH**
00126943 ....$17.99

185. **JAZZ FUSION**
00127558 ....$17.99

186. **JOE PASS**
00128391 ....$16.99

187. **CHRISTMAS FAVORITES**
00128393 ....$16.99

188. **PIAZZOLLA – 10 FAVORITE TUNES**
48023253 ....$16.99

189. **JOHN LENNON**
00138678 ....$16.99

For complete songlists and more visit
halleonard.com

*These do not include split tracks.

JAZZ INSTRUCTION & IMPROVISATION

BOOKS FOR ALL INSTRUMENTS FROM HAL LEONARD

500 JAZZ LICKS
by Brent Vaartstra

This book aims to assist you on your journey to play jazz fluently. These short phrases and ideas we call "licks" will help you understand how to navigate the common chords and chord progressions you will encounter. Adding this vocabulary to your arsenal will send you down the right path and improve your jazz playing, regardless of your instrument.

00142384 ....$16.99

1001 JAZZ LICKS
by Jack Shneidman
Cherry Lane Music

This book presents 1,001 melodic gems played over dozens of the most important chord progressions heard in jazz. This is the ideal book for beginners seeking a well-organized, easy-to-follow encyclopedia of jazz vocabulary, as well as professionals who want to take their knowledge of the jazz language to new heights.

02500133 ....$14.99

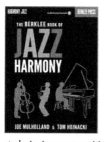

THE BERKLEE BOOK OF JAZZ HARMONY
by Joe Mulholland & Tom Hojnacki

Learn jazz harmony, as taught at Berklee College of Music. This text provides a strong foundation in harmonic principles, supporting further study in jazz composition, arranging, and improvisation. It covers basic chord types and their tensions, with practical demonstrations of how they are used in characteristic jazz contexts and an accompanying recording that lets you hear how they can be applied.

00113755 Book/Online Audio.....................................$19.99

BUILDING A JAZZ VOCABULARY
By Mike Steinel

A valuable resource for learning the basics of jazz from Mike Steinel of the University of North Texas. It covers: the basics of jazz • how to build effective solos • a comprehensive practice routine • and a jazz vocabulary of the masters.

00849911 ....$19.99

COMPREHENSIVE TECHNIQUE FOR JAZZ MUSICIANS
2ND EDITION
by Bert Ligon
Houston Publishing

An incredible presentation of the most practical exercises an aspiring jazz student could want. All are logically interwoven with fine "real world" examples from jazz to classical. This book is an essential anthology of technical, compositional, and theoretical exercises, with lots of musical examples.

00030455 ....$34.99

EAR TRAINING
by Keith Wyatt,
Carl Schroeder and Joe Elliott
Musicians Institute Press

Covers: basic pitch matching • singing major and minor scales • identifying intervals • transcribing melodies and rhythm • identifying chords and progressions • seventh chords and the blues • modal interchange, chromaticism, modulation • and more.

00695198 Book/Online Audio....................................$24.99

EXERCISES AND ETUDES FOR THE JAZZ INSTRUMENTALIST
by J.J. Johnson

Designed as study material and playable by any instrument, these pieces run the gamut of the jazz experience, featuring common and uncommon time signatures and keys, and styles from ballads to funk. They are progressively graded so that both beginners and professionals will be challenged by the demands of this wonderful music.

00842018 Bass Clef Edition $19.99
00842042 Treble Clef Edition $16.95

HOW TO PLAY FROM A REAL BOOK
by Robert Rawlins

Explore, understand, and perform the songs in real books with the techniques in this book. Learn how to analyze the form and harmonic structure, insert an introduction, interpret the melody, improvise on the chords, construct bass lines, voice the chords, add substitutions, and more. It addresses many aspects of solo and small band performance that can improve your own playing and your understanding of what others are doing around you.

00312097 ....$19.99

JAZZ DUETS
ETUDES FOR PHRASING AND ARTICULATION
by Richard Lowell
Berklee Press

With these 27 duets in jazz and jazz-influenced styles, you will learn how to improve your ear, sense of timing, phrasing, and your facility in bringing theoretical principles into musical expression. Covers: jazz staccato & legato • scales, modes & harmonies • phrasing within and between measures • swing feel • and more.

00302151 ....$14.99

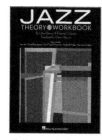

JAZZ THEORY & WORKBOOK
by Lilian Dericq &
Étienne Guéreau

Designed for all instrumentalists, this book teaches how jazz standards are constructed. It is also a great resource for arrangers and composers seeking new writing tools. While some of the musical examples are pianistic, this book is not exclusively for keyboard players.

00159022 ....$19.99

JAZZ THEORY RESOURCES
by Bert Ligon
Houston Publishing, Inc.

This is a jazz theory text in two volumes. **Volume 1 includes:** review of basic theory • rhythm in jazz performance • triadic generalization • diatonic harmonic progressions and analysis • substitutions and turnarounds • and more. **Volume 2 includes:** modes and modal frameworks • quartal harmony • extended tertian structures and triadic superimposition • pentatonic applications • coloring "outside" the lines and beyond • and more.

00030458 Volume 1 ....$39.99
00030459 Volume 2 ....$32.99

JAZZOLOGY
THE ENCYCLOPEDIA OF JAZZ THEORY FOR ALL MUSICIANS
by Robert Rawlins and
Nor Eddine Bahha

This comprehensive resource covers a variety of jazz topics, for beginners and pros of any instrument. The book serves as an encyclopedia for reference, a thorough methodology for the student, and a workbook for the classroom.

00311167 ....$24.99

MODALOGY
SCALES, MODES & CHORDS: THE PRIMORDIAL BUILDING BLOCKS OF MUSIC
by Jeff Brent with Schell Barkley

Primarily a music theory reference, this book presents a unique perspective on the origins, interlocking aspects, and usage of the most common scales and modes in occidental music. Anyone wishing to seriously explore the realms of scales, modes, and their real-world functions will find the most important issues dealt with in meticulous detail within these pages.

00312274 ....$24.99

THE SOURCE
THE DICTIONARY OF CONTEMPORARY AND TRADITIONAL SCALES
by Steve Barta

This book serves as an informative guide for people who are looking for good, solid information regarding scales, chords, and how they work together. It provides right and left hand fingerings for scales, chords, and complete inversions. Includes over 20 different scales, each written in all 12 keys.

00240885 ....$19.99

www.halleonard.com

A R T I S T
TRANSCRIPTIONS®

Artist Transcriptions are authentic, note-for-note transcriptions of today's hottest artists in jazz, pop and rock. These outstanding, accurate arrangements are in an easy-to-read format which includes all essential lines. **Artist Transcriptions** can be used to perform, sequence or for reference.

CLARINET
00672423 Buddy De Franco Collection $19.95

FLUTE
00672379 Eric Dolphy Collection.................$19.95
00672582 The Very Best of James Galway .$19.99
00672372 James Moody Collection –
    Sax and Flute $19.95

GUITAR & BASS
00660113 Guitar Style of George Benson....$19.99
00672573 Ray Brown –
    Legendary Jazz Bassist............. $22.99
00672331 Ron Carter Collection..................$19.99
00660115 Al Di Meola –
    Friday Night in San Francisco..... $17.99
00604043 Al Di Meola –
    Music, Words, Pictures $14.95
00125617 Best of Herb Ellis $19.99
00673245 Jazz Style of Tal Farlow $24.99
00699306 Jim Hall – Exploring Jazz Guitar ..$19.99
00672353 The Joe Pass Collection $19.99
00673216 John Patitucci............................ $17.99
00672374 Johnny Smith – Guitar Solos...... $24.99
00672320 Mark Whitfield Guitar Collection..$19.95

PIANO & KEYBOARD
00672338 The Monty Alexander Collection .$19.95
00672487 Monty Alexander Plays Standards $19.95
00672520 Count Basie Collection $19.95
00192307 Bebop Piano Legends.................$19.99
00113680 Blues Piano Legends.................. $22.99
00672526 The Bill Charlap Collection......... $19.99
00278003 A Charlie Brown Christmas........ $17.99
00672439 Cyrus Chestnut Collection $19.95
00672300 Chick Corea – Paint the World....$19.99
00146105 Bill Evans – Alone...................... $19.99
00672548 The Mastery of Bill Evans $16.99
00672425 Bill Evans – Piano Interpretations $22.99
00672365 Bill Evans – Play Standards....... $22.99
00121885 Bill Evans – Time Remembered ..$19.99
00672510 Bill Evans Trio Vol. 1: 1959-1961 .$27.99
00672511 Bill Evans Trio Vol. 2: 1962-1965..$27.99
00672512 Bill Evans Trio Vol. 3: 1968-1974. $29.99
00672513 Bill Evans Trio Vol. 4: 1979-1980. $24.95
00193332 Erroll Garner –
    Concert by the Sea.................... $22.99
00672486 Vince Guaraldi Collection............$19.99
00289644 The Definitive Vince Guaraldi..... $34.99
00672419 Herbie Hancock Collection......... $22.99
00672438 Hampton Hawes Collection.........$19.95

00672322 Ahmad Jamal Collection $24.99
00255671 Jazz Piano Masterpieces............$19.99
00124367 Jazz Piano Masters Play
    Rodgers & Hammerstein $19.99
00672564 Best of Jeff Lorber...................... $19.99
00672476 Brad Mehldau Collection............ $22.99
00672388 Best of Thelonious Monk $22.99
00672389 Thelonious Monk Collection....... $24.99
00672390 Thelonious Monk Plays
    Jazz Standards – Volume 1 .... $22.99
00672391 Thelonious Monk Plays
    Jazz Standards – Volume 2 .... $22.99
00672433 Jelly Roll Morton –
    The Piano Rolls $17.99
00672553 Charlie Parker Piano featuring
    The Paul Smith Trio (Book/CD)..$19.95
00264094 Oscar Peterson – Night Train $19.99
00672544 Oscar Peterson – Originals.........$14.99
00672531 Oscar Peterson –
    Plays Duke Ellington $24.99
00672563 Oscar Peterson –
    A Royal Wedding Suite $19.99
00672569 Oscar Peterson – Tracks.............$19.99
00672533 Oscar Peterson – Trios...............$29.99
00672534 Very Best of Oscar Peterson...... $22.95
00672371 Bud Powell Classics................... $22.99
00672376 Bud Powell Collection $24.99
00672507 Gonzalo Rubalcaba Collection ...$19.95
00672303 Horace Silver Collection............. $24.99
00672316 Art Tatum Collection $24.99
00672355 Art Tatum Solo Book $19.99
00672357 The Billy Taylor Collection $24.95
00673215 McCoy Tyner $22.99
00672321 Cedar Walton Collection $19.95
00672519 Kenny Werner Collection.............$19.95
00672434 Teddy Wilson Collection $22.99

SAXOPHONE
00672566 The Mindi Abair Collection $14.99
00673244 Julian "Cannonball"
    Adderley Collection $22.99
00673237 Michael Brecker $19.99
00672429 Michael Brecker Collection $24.99
00672394 James Carter Collection.............$19.95
00672529 John Coltrane – Giant Steps.......$17.99
00672494 John Coltrane – A Love Supreme$16.99
00672493 John Coltrane Plays
    "Coltrane Changes".....................$19.95
00672453 John Coltrane Plays Standards.. $24.99
00673233 John Coltrane Solos $27.99
00672328 Paul Desmond Collection...........$19.99
00672530 Kenny Garrett Collection $22.99

00699375 Stan Getz.....................................$19.99
00672377 Stan Getz – Bossa Novas $22.99
00672375 Stan Getz – Standards $19.99
00673254 Great Tenor Sax Solos $22.99
00672523 Coleman Hawkins Collection $22.99
00672330 Best of Joe Henderson $24.99
00673239 Best of Kenny G......................... $22.99
00673229 Kenny G – Breathless $19.99
00672462 Kenny G –
    Classics in the Key of G............. $22.99
00672485 Kenny G – Faith: A Holiday Album. $17.99
00672373 Kenny G – The Moment $19.99
00672498 Jackie McLean Collection $19.95
00672372 James Moody Collection –
    Sax and Flute $19.95
00672416 Frank Morgan Collection $19.95
00672539 Gerry Mulligan Collection........... $22.99
00672561 Best of Sonny Rollins..................$19.95
00102751 Sonny Rollins, Art Blakey & Kenny Drew
    with the Modern Jazz Quartet $17.95
00675000 David Sanborn Collection $19.99
00672528 The Bud Shank Collection $19.95
00672491 The New Best of Wayne Shorter $24.99
00672550 The Sonny Stitt Collection...........$19.95
00672524 Lester Young Collection...............$19.99

TROMBONE
00672332 J.J. Johnson Collection $22.99
00672489 Steve Turré Collection $19.99

TRUMPET
00672557 Herb Alpert Collection................ $19.99
00672480 Louis Armstrong Collection $19.99
00672481 Louis Armstrong Plays Standards$19.99
00672435 Chet Baker Collection $22.99
00672556 Best of Chris Botti $19.99
00672448 Miles Davis – Originals, Vol. 1.....$19.99
00672451 Miles Davis – Originals, Vol. 2.....$19.95
00672449 Miles Davis – Standards, Vol. 2...$19.95
00672479 Dizzy Gillespie Collection $19.95
00673214 Freddie Hubbard $19.99
00672506 Chuck Mangione Collection........$19.99
00672525 Arturo Sandoval –
    Trumpet Evolution $19.99

HAL•LEONARD®

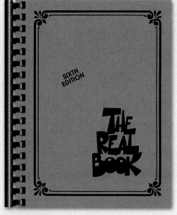